"Swipe Up is sane, funny, hones̶ ̶ ̶ ̶ ̶ ̶ ̶ ̶
Jason Roach does a marvello̶ ̶ ̶ ̶ ̶ ̶ ̶ ̶
vision for sexuality in our br̶c̶ ̶ ̶ ̶ ̶ ̶ ̶
and completely recognisable. It's both sensitive and ̶ ̶ ̶ ̶ ̶ ̶
one—married or single, Christian or not-Christian—could read *Swipe Up* without laughing, rethinking or even shedding a tear. Read it, talk about it, pass it on!"

GARY MILLAR; Principal, Queensland
Theological College, Australia

"In a world where our Western culture's narrative about sex and relationships so easily steals our minds, this little gem of a book helps us lift our gaze and see a far more beautiful story. Seamlessly weaving together personal experience and biblical truth, Jason Roach reminds us of God's astonishing love and the privilege it is to love others in ways that honour him. It's not a book of "don'ts" but a book that helps us rejoice in our risen Lord. Accessible, practical and wonderfully engaging—a great read for anyone desiring purity, intimacy and joy."

HELEN THORNE; Director of Training and Mentoring,
London City Mission; Author, *Purity is Possible*

"This week you'll be gazing at numerous screens that reinforce our culture's fantasies of love, sex and relationships. Why not give up some of that time to gaze at the reality of God and his better love stories? Reading Jason's personal and practical book will do you so much more good."

ED SHAW; Pastor; Co-founder, livingout.org;
Author, *The Plausibility Problem*

"Jason Roach must have swallowed a truth pill to write this book! It's so real about intimacy, loneliness, adolescence, singleness, marriage and friendship. Amid the searing honesty, he shows us how he discovered an amazing map that enabled him and can help us to stay clear of the storms. It's a map and a story you'd be mad to miss. I'll be thoroughly recommending it across the generations at All Souls."

RICO TICE; Senior Minister, All Souls Langham Place, London;
Founder of Christianity Explored Ministries

"Jason tells his story of finding real intimacy through his life experiences and faith. God has a purpose for our lives that we need to discover through his Son. This wonderful book invites us to find true, long-lasting, fulfilling, intimate love through Jesus Christ."

DR KAROWEI DORGU; Bishop of Woolwich

"Jason helpfully gives us biblical truth and pastoral wisdom, wrapped up in a deeply honest and personal narrative. Rather than confront, he gently persuades us that God offers a better way of navigating the pitfalls of modern romance and relationships."

**MATT FULLER; Senior Minister, Christ Church, Mayfair, London;
Author, *Perfect Sinners***

"I'm very thankful for this book, and I couldn't recommend it more highly. Jason is both honest and realistic while also being witty and practical. This is a book for both single and married people alike, because no matter who we are or where we're at in life, we all need pointing to God's better story for our lives, and Jason does exactly that."

RACHELL MICHELL; Family and Youth Worker, South London

"Here is a gem of a little book explaining why God's blueprint for our sexuality isn't limiting but is actually liberating. Jason combines his personal story with powerful and pastoral application. And because it's accessible and concise, it's the kind of book you can buy, read and pass on."

MARTIN SALTER; Bedford Community Church; Editor, *Foundations*

"This book is deeply honest, real and human. Jason reflects on his own story through the lens of his faith in Jesus. He opens up a conversation about sex, relationships, intimacy and holiness. It is a conversation that the whole church needs to be having. This book will encourage you and challenge you, and at all times it will point you to Jesus."

**KATE WHARTON; Vicar of St. Bart's Roby, Liverpool;
Assistant National Leader, New Wine**

"Jason is so honest, clear and real. He gets who we are and who God is. I love 'thanks, sorry, please and never' as a summary of the Bible on sex and the sexual revolution. It's a great read, and you'll be reading it again and giving it away to all your friends."

KEITH SINCLAIR; Bishop of Birkenhead

JASON ROACH

Swipe Up

A better way to do love,
sex and relationships

thegoodbook
COMPANY

Swipe Up
© Jason Roach, 2019

Published by:
The Good Book Company

thegoodbook.com | www.thegoodbook.co.uk
thegoodbook.com.au | thegoodbook.co.nz | thegoodbook.co.in

Unless indicated, all Scripture references are taken from the Holy Bible, New International Version. Copyright © 2011 Biblica. Used by permission.

A CIP catalogue record for this book is available from the British Library.

Jason Roach has asserted his right under the Copyright, Designs and Patents Act 1988 to be identified as author of this work.

ISBN: 9781784983703 | Printed in the UK

Design by André Parker

Contents

Foreword

Glynn Harrison
Psychiatrist and author of A Better Story

This is a big book. Not because it's long or very detailed—you could get through it in an evening. Not because it brings to life the Bible's teaching about sex and relationships in a different way, although it does that. Not even because it's a page-turner (and it is).

It's big because *it's real*. It's about life. It's about you and me.

The new attitude to love, sex and relationships in our culture has been a massive wake-up call to Christians who want to take the Bible seriously. It has exposed our shallow teaching and pastoral care in the area of sex and relationships; it has called out our hypocrisies and flushed out our culture of shame. People are telling us they know what Christians are against—but what are we *for*?

In contrast to the fear and shame offered by religion, the sexual revolution gives us stories of justice and equality. It casts a grand narrative of freedom from the straightjacketing shame from small-minded bigots with their boundaries and rules. Over and over again it gives us stories with the same happy ending—the liberation of just "being yourself". *What's not to like about that?*

In my book *A Better Story* I argued that you can't respond to a good story with facts. You need to tell a *different* story. Christians need to rediscover and to tell our own story, which is at the heart of the Bible—a life-giving story of how humans truly flourish as we learn to live in harmony with our design. And then we need to tell that story in ways that connect with hearts as well as minds. We need to signal that we get what our culture is saying to us about oppression, abuse, hypocrisy and shame. We need to acknowledge the questions before we rush out the answers. That is what this book sets out to do.

Jason brings a unique set of skills to the task. Because of his background, he knows something about the issues surrounding "inclusion". He's a doctor who knows about the body and how sex works. He's a Christian minister, working in a challenging urban context. He knows about kids, because he has four of his own. And as an advisor to the Bishop of London, his voice is heard in other corridors as well.

We owe him a great debt. With so much going on, Jason has carved out time to tell us his story, which starts with a pole dancer and ends with the Saviour. He inspires us to imagine that following the Jesus way can leave us feeling more fully alive than ever we imagined.

Swipe up

She walked into the room, took off her coat and looked over at me. One smile and I was utterly transfixed. Her mouth was moving, but I had no idea what she was saying. I was charged; magnetically pulled towards her. On the stage of my life, a spotlight had just lit her up and I was the only person in the audience. As crazy as it seemed, all I wanted to do was step up from my seat and join her in the light. So I did.

But if that part of the journey proved easy, the voyage that followed wasn't.

Going out with her was often hard work for me. There were days when it felt like a huge struggle to keep my hands off her. At other times though, making basic conversation felt exhausting. When it came to handling intimacy, I was all over the place.

I first met the woman I am now married to in the days before dating apps had become popular and widespread. But as a teenager and as a younger man, I conformed to all the stereotypes of the day. While I was hungry for genuine love, affection and meaningful intimacy, I was also laddish and shallow. On meeting girls, I would mentally *swipe left* (not for me) or *swipe right* (I'm interested) and instantly drop people into categories based on what *I* wanted.

But then there would come the rare moment when the fireworks went off. I would meet someone and "super-like" them. *Swipe up.*

I guess I'm a romantic at heart, but when you meet someone like that, you're no longer just flirting for fun. The stakes are much higher; the implications reach much deeper inside you. There is the possibility of scary, deeply affecting life-changing intimacy.

The problem we all have

By intimacy, I mean that experience of affection when you are with someone. We can experience intimacy in many different ways: catching up with a lifelong pal, meeting someone for the first time, or enjoying a special time with a group of friends or with a lover. Experiencing intimacy can be fun and fiery. Heart-racing magnetism makes our hairs stand on end. And yet at other times it's frightening and frustrating. We can feel unsettled, out of our depth and desperately alone.

This book is about how we navigate the choppy, turbulent waters of intimacy, whatever our relationship status. We all have an instinct to head for the fireworks and steer clear of the storms. Yet, often we're just not sure what that looks like. If God is our compass in life and relationships, we struggle to work out which way He's pointing.

I want to share the story of how, as a Christian, I came to hear God's voice and let him direct me through the exhilarating, terrifying waves of intimacy.

That last sentence might make you feel nervous. After all, it is so different from the message of our culture. That message seems to be that we should set our own course—"set sail in your own direction". In other words, do what feels right for you—*follow your heart*. So what happens if God's direction feels like stepping out of your skin? What if *his* direction is the opposite of what your heart is saying?

Our fear

I've experienced that concern myself, both before and after starting to follow Jesus. I've found myself thinking, when it comes to intimacy—do I want guidance at all? But a couple of things have kept me coming back to God.

First, I've made some monster mistakes in life—and frustratingly I seem to keep making them! My mistakes remind me that relying on my own judgement doesn't always end well. The truth is that sometimes I just don't know what is best for me or those around me.

The second thing is the flip-side of this. Getting the best advice available can help me make up my own mind. For example, I find that it's generally worth listening to what my doctor has to say, even when I'd rather not. To chart the best course in life, I need the wisdom of others.

An opportunity

Now, what if you could access wisdom for intimacy that was more reliable than a doctor's diagnosis? What if someone knew our situations better than we did and could tell us the best way to navigate? And what if that route meant we could head for the fireworks and steer clear of the storms? I believe that God has provided that wisdom. His words have energised me to approach the search for intimacy with joy.

I've discovered that all of us are part of a shared story of God's love. It's this story that has given me the power to grow a satisfying life of love through all of the different stages of my life.

I don't want to mislead you about myself or this book—because my journey has been complicated and messy. Of course there have been setbacks along the way, because doing life, whatever situation you are in, is tough. But God's story lights up a path through the turbulent waters of intimacy.

An invitation

I want to invite you to sail with me on a journey through my experiences of intimacy in my teenage life, a period of singleness as a young adult, and now in marriage. You might be in any one of those life stages. A teenager just trying to work out your feelings. A single person battling with loneliness. A married person struggling for contentment. Whoever you are, I hope that you find something here that speaks to you.

The details of your particular journey will be different from mine. I am a black British man in my mid thirties, married with young children. I grew up in the nineties and noughties in south London, with all the cultural baggage that comes with that. You will be different. I apologise if what I say comes across as laddish towards women—I'm just being honest about what I was, and the things I struggled with then, and continue to struggle with now.

But, different though we are, the Bible leads me to believe that the shape of our struggles will overlap—we all connect with this very basic human experience. We long for intimacy with it's agonies and the ecstasies.

My biggest prayer for you, as you read this book, is that God's story might light up a path through the troubled waters for you.

1. Something more?

or My girlfriend was a pole dancer

Saturday afternoon along Bromley High Street was a kind of catwalk for teenagers. It was where you went to hang out, even though the only real place of interest to a sixteen-year-old with not a lot of money to their name was McDonalds. And so the focus as we lined up—apart from French fries—was one another.

There were *the untouchables*—the group you never went near for fear of being ridiculed (or lynched). There was *the cool crew,* who were always rockin' the latest Air Jordans; you hoped they would acknowledge you (in my case in vain). There were *the geeks,* who had their own brand of cool and who generally kept themselves to themselves.

And then there was *me*, a South London schoolkid trying to find his way. Definitely more *geek* than *cool*, but not particularly fitting in with any of them.

But on this particular Saturday I was strutting... *Why?* Because I was walking along with my girlfriend. She was tall, dark and lovely. As we walked along, the spotlight was on me, and for once I didn't care. Holding her hand made my skin tingle, my chest pout and my own personal central-heating system kick in on full power. Bring on the catwalk. Life felt good.

I was "in love", and I wasn't afraid to tell people about it—even her mother. I remember her face to this day when I declared my adoration for her daughter in front of her.

A restrained disbelief that melted into laughter. Looking back I can understand her reaction. But whether love was the right name for it or not, the sense of intoxicating connection with this astonishing creature was utterly real.

And then it broke.

The bubble bursts

We were at a house party together—the throbbing beat from the basement dance floor satisfyingly shaking the whole house. I'd come up to street level to welcome a mate who had just arrived. As we bantered, I felt a tug at my hoodie. There was a touch of aggression that made me spin round. Another friend whispered in my ear and beckoned me back downstairs.

I arrived at the makeshift dance floor to see my girlfriend in the middle, shamelessly playing tonsil tennis with another guy.

As I stared at her and half the room stared back at me, the euphoric bubble I'd happily been floating in for the past few weeks exploded in a shower of conflicting feelings. It felt like when the landlord turns all the lights on in the pub at the end of the evening. You are hit by stark reality. Our relationship had seemed stable, sweet and serene, but now all I could see was two sweaty bodies and my own stupidity. She wasn't perfect after all. And apparently, neither was I.

Aftermath

Things dragged along for a little while after that. By now, we'd been together for years and surely it wasn't worth throwing everything away over that one incident. Plus, she'd said "sorry" with a doe-eyed look of remorse that was hard to resist.

I pretended that everything was fine, but it wasn't. Sparks had flown between us, I'd made myself vulnerable and now I'd been burnt. I felt foolish and hurt. At the same time I was afraid to let on just how much it bothered me for fear of losing what had seemed so special.

A few weeks later our relationship took a completely unexpected turn. We were walking down the road where she lived towards the high street, as we often did on a Saturday afternoon. The sun was shining, car stereos were booming, and we skipped along to the beats. It was then that she broke the news, out of the blue, in a matter-of-fact kind of way. She wanted to become a pole dancer.

Her reasons were simple. She had worked out that she could earn better money pole dancing *right now* than many university graduates did. Plus she would cut out the hassle of student debt and study too. And she got to spend the rest of the day shopping. To be clear, she didn't have to do this because she was hard up or in dire straits. It was just a life choice. She hadn't broken stride for a moment during this revelation. In her mind there was nothing remotely unusual about her conclusions.

Now she slowed and looked over at me, looking for some kind of affirmation. My mind was momentarily paralysed. And in retrospect I was glad. I'm not sure I would have said anything constructive. Her new path of freedom left me confused and hurt. Why were these incidents so bruising to me and yet almost insignificant to her?

Assumptions

I realised that there was a huge assumption in my mind about relationships that we didn't share. My assumption was that if you were dedicated to someone emotionally, you would be dedicated to them physically as well. For me, the fact that she was okay with sharing her body with others meant that our emotional connection, despite appearances, was not okay after all.

We soon parted ways. But the truth is that I pined for her and for more of those feelings that brought us together in the first place—that desire for closeness.

I wasn't alone. A desire for intimacy was clear to see among my friends in all kinds of ways. Endless Friday-night binge drinking, hoping for some "action"; endless piles of lads' magazines; endless pursuit of the "well done" from our teachers and bosses. And then Monday would roll around again, and none of us felt any closer to being satisfied.

Not that we'd have put it into words like that. But looking back on it, the treadmill of our lives told its own story. Somehow the intimacy we were searching for appeared to be tantalisingly close. The parties, the personalities on the covers of the magazines, and the people whose affirmation we craved all seemed to be offering it. Yet at the same time, it also seemed mysteriously out of reach.

I shouldn't have supersized

Fast forward to the final stretch of A-levels. I was walking out of a head-spinning physics lesson when a new student ambled across my path. The spinning in my head did an emergency stop. She was stunning. So much so that in the weeks that followed I found it hard to be near her. It felt like just to approach her would pollute the airspace.

It took a mate of mine weeks to cajole me into asking her to go to McDonalds for a milkshake. Finally, heart pumping, sweat pouring, I popped the question. She said yes.

But the date was far less charged than I expected. As we started eating, I was struggling to find words to say. As the silences lengthened, I found myself painfully aware of what each customer was ordering at the till behind us. With each completed order the nervousness ramped up. She was struggling too.

It wasn't that we didn't want to get to know each other, but it felt like there was a mountain of awkwardness to climb to get to the point of really talking to each other. We didn't make it through half the milkshake before I was left to go solo with my cold quarter pounder.

I'd never really stopped to think about it before, but at this point in my life all kinds of ideas were flying around my brain. If sex and relationships were what life was all about—and that's what the TV, lads' mags and my mates at the time agreed on—then why was it so hard to open up to people?

I'd reached the age where I was free to explore relationships. But why did the ones that went pear-shaped leave me with so much pain? Perhaps you've asked these questions before. Or as you read them now, you remember your own painful teenage experiences and wonder about them too.

Processing passion

I was watching TV recently when a perfume advert came on featuring Natalie Portman. It started with her taking off her sunglasses in a sultry pose and licking the end of them. Then came a high-speed montage of her shouting at her boyfriend, jumping off a bridge into the sea, her boyfriend chasing her around her flat and then both of them running along the beach looking insanely happy before jumping out of a red sports car, looking into the camera and asking, "What would you do for love?"

It was an electric picture of high-intensity passion but also freedom from restraint. And it was captivating. It felt like I was being invited into a life of joy. The way in was simply to be sexually unshackled from people's expectations—and to buy their overpriced scent of course. This was the story about relationships that I was learning as a teenager from the world around me and is still very much our society's story today. I wanted in then, and this story's selling power has not diminished with time.

So far it had seemed beyond my reach. I craved relationships full of high-intensity passion, and yet the reality was that high intensity-passion seemed to take time as you slowly began to understand someone. Then the small measure of "passion" that I managed to muster in relationships seemed to come at a huge price. I was vulnerable to hurt, like when my girlfriend decided to become a pole dancer. But I was not going to let those hiccups deter me.

Grown-up girlfriend

A few years later I met someone at work. It had been easy to get to know her in the run of office life. We'd sneak out for coffee and lose track of time. Conversation was easy. Chemistry was powerful. But as our relationship was starting to blossom, I was also learning what it meant to be in a relationship with Jesus.

A group of friends had invited me along to some church events, and I'd begun to read the Bible. As I read and listened, I was blown away by the words and ways of the risen Jesus and got involved with a church. Two relationships were growing side by side.

I hadn't grown up belonging to a local church, and everything felt a little strange, but the community was kind and welcomed me in. One evening, a small group of us were meeting to hang out and have a look at the Bible together. I was waxing lyrical about my newfound love, and one of the other Christians there began to lovingly probe. Was she a believer? Had we had sex? Did I have marriage in mind? It became clear in an inescapable way that I wasn't going about things the Christian way.

I went home and wept.

And then I broke up with her.

I knew in my head that this was what God wanted me to do. But my heart was in a different place. It felt like my body was saying *Yes!* to this relationship, but that Jesus was giving a resounding *No!* I felt frustrated with myself for feeling drawn to disobey God and frustrated with God for saying no to what felt so natural and good.

I know my story is not unique. So many Christians today feel this way: hungry for relationships and yet torn between how we feel and what our faith seems to demand. It's made harder by crazy, uninhibited love stories like the one portrayed in the perfume ad.

They shout out *passion and pleasure come only as you plough your own path to sexual freedom.*

And often our solution as individuals and as churches is to try and bury our heads in the sand. We want to just forget about it and hope that the problem will go away, but it won't. And to those who are struggling and to an incredulous watching world, the silence is deafening.

I want to suggest that hoping that our feelings will go away is the wrong thing to do. What changed things for me was realising that I hadn't grasped the fullness of the Christian story. God has taken me on a journey of discovery in this area of relationships. I've discovered that it's not a choice between passion-free faith and sensual fun. That is not the Christian story. What's more, God has not left us in the dark about what that story is. Instead he's mapped it out in his big story told in the scriptures. It has grown my love for Jesus and so enriched my faith.

And bottom line: I think his story not only makes sense but is *better* than the story the world is telling us.

2. Here for a reason

or How shaving has never been quite the same again

When it came to relationships, at this point in my life, I felt like a reluctant believer. I wanted to follow Jesus, but felt that on the issue of sexuality, Jesus simply didn't get the human condition. Christianity seemed to be saying, "Deny what you feel". And that felt both hard and harsh. It looked like God had conjured up a set of arbitrary rules simply to spoil our fun.

It took me a while to get beyond this. But I came to see that I'd got it backwards. Christianity wasn't saying, "Deny what you feel" but "Dig deeper". God's rules weren't arbitrary but purposeful. I want to unpack that story some more.

The big picture
I was still finding my way as a Christian when I had the opportunity go along to a "Bible overview" course

at church. We surveyed the big story of the Bible over several weeks. It was there that I first began to see that the Bible was a love story. It wasn't "Twelve rules for life" or a spiritual "get out of jail free" card but more like an epic retelling of *Romeo and Juliet* that took place across the stars. A love story in which God puts his life on the line for his bride.

Up to this point, I had thought of God as a Saviour, yes, but predominantly as a judge or a policeman. I imagined that if God was assessing me on an app, one look at my ugly thoughts and self-serving motivations would provoke an instant swipe left: *rejection*.

But as we worked through the Bible story, I discovered to my astonishment that God is revealed, first and foremost, not as an angry judge but as *a lover*. In spite of everything I think and do, his first instinct is not just to give me a begrudging swipe right, but to swipe up with passion and commitment.

Our Maker is described as our husband (Isaiah 54 v 5), and to be unfaithful to him is described as adultery (Hosea 1 v 2). In other words, when God wants to describe the intensity of his love for his people, he doesn't hesitate to use the language of a sexual relationship. It seems that only this kind of language can begin to capture the intensity of love that God offers us.

I began to realise that God had crafted creation to show us what he was like. He had made *me* with all the interests, passions and capabilities I have so that I could discover God. Love was meant to lead me to the Lord.

My sixteen-year-old "can't take my eyes [or hands] off of you" euphoria over my new girlfriend was a sign. The wonder that made my heart skip a beat outside the physics lesson was a sign. The chemistry in the coffee shop that left me feeling intoxicated with joy was a sign. These experiences were all signposts pointing to the dizzy heights of God's love.

Perhaps there are moments when you have known something like this. When you have spotted someone walking towards you and felt like dancing (even if only on the inside). Or a song on the radio has opened a window into a moment of past passion. All these moments are meant to point us to a deeper reality: the love story that God has put on display in the saving work of Jesus.

Running from love

I had already discovered that the big stumbling block to enjoying God's love was our broken relationship with him. What was new was one of the fundamental ways that we experience that brokenness: *we find it hard to be honest with each other.*

When God made the first human beings, they were on good terms with him: in a right relationship. The Bible account tells us that, at this point, they were naked and yet "felt no shame" (Genesis 2 v 25). There was no need to hide anything from God. They could let him know who they really were and know that it was going to be okay. And this was the same openness they enjoyed with each other.

But when they turned away from him, all that changed. Now they were naked *and* ashamed. They wanted to hide, not just from him but from each other (3 v 7-8). Although they still wanted to be close, they were scared of letting anyone know what they were really like. They feared rejection.

As I read these words on the very first pages of the Bible, suddenly my McDonalds moment came flooding back to me. That moment of finding it tough to be honest with someone close stemmed from my broken relationship with God. That moment and a thousand other McDonalds moments were part of something bigger—signposts to a bigger problem than teenage angst.

So often with those closest to me, it was the struggle to share how I really felt that made the relationships so hard. I felt the need to hide the fact that I didn't really know what they were talking about, or that I was ashamed of something in my past, or that something they had done had really annoyed me, in fear that it might drive them away.

What lies beneath

The more I thought about it, the more I realised that hiding was, in subtle ways, a chronic problem. And now I saw where it came from—our turning away from God. He had hardwired me for relationships. But I would always struggle to get those horizontal relationships right with others until I got my vertical relationship with God right. That got me excited about digging deeper.

The good news was that God's love story was all about how he'd acted in history to fix this brokenness. And at the centre of it all was an other-worldly wedding. It was a story about how Jesus put his life on the line to win back his wayward bride. Marriage was God's ultimate picture of his passionate, faithful and life-giving love.

As we combed the pages of the Bible, we discovered that it brimmed over with potent imagery of God's love. He was like a father, a mother, a shepherd, a friend. But more common than any of those images was marriage. The passionate love of God was like that of a bridegroom who "rejoices over his bride" (Isaiah 62 v 5). The faithfulness of God's love was declared to us with a "solemn oath" (Ezekiel 16 v 8). The life-giving love of God, who created us in the first place (Genesis 1 v 27), found its most fitting picture in the union of a husband and wife.

And this is how the big story ends. The last book in the Bible pictures eternity as an enormous wedding banquet with Christ and his beautiful bride, where there is intimacy, celebration and "happily ever after":

Then I heard what sounded like a great multitude, like the roar of rushing waters and like loud peals of thunder, shouting:
"Hallelujah!
For our Lord God Almighty reigns.

Let us rejoice and be glad
   and give him glory!
For the wedding of the Lamb has come,
   and his bride has made herself ready.
Fine linen, bright and clean,
   was given her to wear."
(Fine linen stands for the righteous acts of God's holy
people.)

Then the angel said to me, "Write this: 'Blessed are those
who are invited to the wedding supper of the Lamb!'"
And he added, "These are the true words of God".
                                          (Revelation 19 v 6-9)

God's passionate love was what the joy and excitement
and fun of the perfume ad was ultimately pointing to. His
faithful love was what my pole-dancing girlfriend made
me yearn for. His life-giving love was what I'd experienced
as my parents nurtured me. And yet I had discovered
that naturally we run away from his love. The result is
frustrated relationships in which we hide who we really
are from each other. We are naked and ashamed.

Displaying love

God's love is not simply pictured as a marriage for us
to look at but as a story for us to live in and live out. In
other words, we are meant to put God's love on display.
The Bible begins with a marriage between Adam and Eve
and ends with a marriage between Jesus and his people.
These bookends of the Bible not only point to what God's

love is like, but also to the fact that we were made to put this story on display to the world. In other words, God designed the world so that what he is doing cosmically will be mirrored in the detail of your life and relationships.

Marriage is the clearest and most obvious way in which we love as he loves. This doesn't rule out other forms of love. But God has etched marriage into human flesh as the best picture of the love story he has with us. He puts this pretty plainly in Ephesians 5:

> *Husbands, love your wives, just as Christ loved the church and gave himself up for her to make her holy, cleansing her by the washing with water through the word, and to present her to himself as a radiant church, without stain or wrinkle or any other blemish, but holy and blameless.*
> *(Ephesians 5 v 25-27)*

Who I am

So God is a lover who has made us to love as he loves, "just as Christ loved the church." This took time for me to grasp. It was a huge shift in thinking. But one of the things that helped me most was realising that in the Bible sex isn't about following arbitrary rules but about flourishing according to my design—being who I truly am.

This was because we were designed to be God's royal representatives—like the Duke and Duchess of Cambridge acting on behalf of the Queen, but with much bigger job descriptions. Right at the beginning of God's love story we are told that human beings were made "in the image of God" (Genesis 1 v 26-27). This term would have meant "royal representative" to the first hearers because kings of the ancient world were referred to as "the image of the Gods," heavenly representatives on earth. Incredibly, the God of the Bible has declared that when it comes to representing him, we are all "the image of God". Every human being is an ambassador.

One Saturday morning I was dragged along to a cooked breakfast at my local church. "Dragged" is probably a little strong considering that bacon was on offer. Someone got up to speak for a few minutes while we filled our faces. The thing that stuck with me was the description of his morning shaving routine. He would take a business card, scribble out the job description and write instead "Ambassador for Christ" and put it on his shaving mirror to reflect on as he scraped at his stubble.

This was an *"aha"* moment for me. Whatever work I happened to be doing, wherever I was in the world, I had a job of monumental importance to do—to be an ambassador for my King.

I was beginning to see what a privilege and responsibility being an image-bearer was. And this meant, in part, that what our relationships look like to others was important. It was not simply about what felt good to us, but what was most fitting for the King we represented. A couple can have all kinds of narratives for their life together—travel, fun, family, growing a business together, feathering a beautiful nest for themselves. But if God is a lover who has made us to love like him, then marriage is fundamentally about something much bigger. It is a way of displaying to the world the three principal hallmarks of his saving love: its passion, faithfulness and life-giving nature—in a unique and special way.

Saying yes to God's story

When it comes to our individual relationships, a married person committed to Christ said *Yes!* to God's story by saying *No!* to the intimate advances of others—in other words, by sticking with their spouse. Just as Jesus sticks with us even at the cost of his life, we stick with our partners. As I looked around in the church I was part of, I began to see the married people in a new way. As they faithfully stuck with one another, they pictured for everyone to see the faithful love of Christ for his people— his bride.

A single person committed to Christ said *Yes!* to God's story by saying *No!* to sex outside of marriage: in other words, by faithful abstinence. Jesus doesn't do one-night stands or fall out of love with his people—so nor do we with him. Again as I looked around, I began to see in a new way the single people living out this call to abstinence. They pointed me to a Christ who was worthy of our total devotion.

So both married and the single people put God's love story on display in different ways. The married person displays the "earthly" part of God's love story—faithfully and sacrificially sticking with their spouse so that they grow and flourish. That's what Jesus did in coming to earth to die for us. The single woman or guy displays the "heavenly" part of God's love story—joyfully focusing on their faithful Saviour. That's what we will do for the rest of forever in heaven. We put this love story on display because God is a lover who made us to love like him—with marriage being the central expression of his passionate, faithful and life-giving love.

What makes a good relationship?

A light-bulb moment for me was how this changed what I understood a good relationship to be. It wasn't simply about me being happy or us as a couple not hurting each other or anyone else. There was a bigger issue. Was I putting God's love story on display, his way? Was I following his blueprint for passionate, faithful, life-giving love?

The Bible didn't ignore the relational brokenness that I saw around me either. I've mentioned the discomfort and struggle I experienced when dating. I'd grown up seeing some of the trials of marriage that my parents had to go through. I'd witnessed the scars of friends who'd survived the car crash of their parents' divorce. It showed me the realistic truth of the statement "The parents eat sour grapes, and the children's teeth are set on edge" (Ezekiel 18 v 2). The Bible is not blind or unrealistic about the realities of life. But it also offers hope. Time and again the

34

biblical narrative cries out *you are not alone*. It documents the lives of people who have walked through the ashes of burnt relationships too, and yet remain loved and protected, and part of God's purposes.

It was also clear to me that even among Christian believers sin could remain rampant. We all know stories of train-wrecks among Christian marriages that looked "perfect" from the outside. The damage is immense, but we weave our way through the wreckage as best we can. No one finds living out this vision of sexuality easy. But the limitations of our obedience don't mean that there are limitations in God's design. His blueprint best displays his goodness and best enables our flourishing, despite our failings.

Singing our own song

I may have made this sound as if it was an easy journey of discovery for me. But the truth is that at the time all this was profoundly disturbing to me, and incredibly difficult to take in. Blueprints can feel oppressive and constraining. My biggest question personally was how, as a single person, I could find the confidence and conviction to keep swimming against the tide in this area. Would I actually be able to live this vision out without imploding?

And yet I was beginning to see that God's commands were not arbitrary. They had a purpose—to display God's passionate, faithful and life-giving love to the world. To give up on his vision for sex was ultimately to give up on him.

So it turns out that the big question about sexuality in the Christian life isn't "What am I allowed to do?" but "Who am I?" If I am God's image-bearer, then seeking to live his way and to follow Jesus is the best way to be true to myself. I could seek a relationship at the expense of my connection to Christ or I could seek Jesus and find that better relationships come thrown in as a bonus.

Voices

It was also a welcome relief. Without really realising it, I had been struggling to work out which voices to listen to. There was the voice of my mates who said "Sow your oats and become a man". There was the voice of the R&B music I listened to which said "Focus on your sex appeal". There was the voice of the movies I watched, that often said "Don't settle for anything less than your one true love, whatever mess that makes along the way". Then there was the voice of the latest lads' mag I happened to have read, which said, "Life consists of rating the women around you based on their anatomy". Swipe left. Swipe right. Swipe up.

Those voices felt like an echo chamber for the themes of perfume ads and pornography. The music that emerged said: "live a sexually unshackled life, free from restrictions". But what exactly that meant was so different from voice to voice that trying to dance to the music felt exhausting. In fact it felt like dancing in a very crowded nightclub. You were trying to enjoy yourself and everyone was smiling at each other, but frankly you felt more shoved than satisfied.

Shoved around by the different ideas and hurt by the emotional fallout that often arose from trying to follow them through. But now I was realising that, all the while, God was singing a different song. I'd managed to tune it out, but it had been there all along. God is a lover who had made us to love like him.

Comforted by love

There was another profound truth that I realised about God's love. While we fail to put it on display perfectly, his passionate love for us never fails. I write this as someone who has messed up in relationships many times. And yet Jesus, knowing how badly I would fail, endured the cross so that I would be able to enjoy him for ever as a forgiven friend. Romans 5 v 8 says "While we were still sinners, Christ died for us". Not only that, but right now he comforts, guides and lovingly leads me every day of my life.

God has allowed me to experience that loving connection in many ways. There have been times when I've been badly let down and have felt completely alone, and yet I have known the precious love of Christ sustaining me. I remember a very low point when I had a catastrophic falling out with my father. At the time he was so angry with me he said that he would never speak to me again. As I put the phone down, I was utterly distraught.

But in that very moment the Lord gave me an overwhelming sense of his comfort. I vividly experienced what Paul described as being "sorrowful and yet always rejoicing" (2 Corinthians 6 v 10). The Spirit of God brought his promises home to me with such power that it overwhelmed me like a flood.

But it hasn't always been like that. There have been plenty of times when I would have loved to have *felt* the supernatural comfort of God and yet, as David writes in some of the psalms, I experienced nothing but emptiness and frustration. I'd ask someone out that I'd fancied for months, but get knocked back and feel overwhelmed with disappointment. I'd replay the phone call in my head over and over again, thinking about how pathetic I sounded. I'd break up with someone I'd been seeing for months and find that being in the same room with them made me shake with sadness.

In those times, thankfully, I've been able to cling with cast-iron confidence to the *facts* about the love of God. His commitment to his lavish love echoes throughout the Scriptures whether I feel it or not. The feelings that I had experienced for others and the feelings that they had shared for me were fickle. There were magnificent peaks, and there were dark valleys. But God's love was richly passionate, reliably faithful and always life-giving. Even when I felt nothing but numbness, I still belonged to him, he still held me powerfully, and he wouldn't let go until I met him face to face (see Psalm 73 v 23-26).

As well as this, God's people in the church have been his physical arms of love around me. A shoulder to cry on, a sounding board to vent my confusion, a sofa to crash on.

As I look back over the years, I'm amazed at all the people God has provided through the church to stand by me. As I experienced the love of God through his word and his people, I began to see the truth of the phrase I had heard people throw out so often: that "God has made us for himself, and our hearts are restless until they find their rest in him".

Rubber meets road

Of course, knowing that we are in God's big story does not immediately solve all our struggles. We still feel ourselves pulled in all directions, because investing in one relationship has all kinds of implications for the other relationships in our lives. Going to a birthday meal with a sibling might mean I can't go to a gig with my friend. Visiting my dad might mean I have to miss a date night with my wife. And it seems that the more precious the relationship, the greater the implications for what we can and can't invest in relationships with others.

But it does help enormously to know that we have one defining story about ourselves around which we will evaluate and work out all the others. Because God's story is the best story, and the one we constantly refer back to, saying *No!* to one thing can actually be part of a much deeper *Yes!* to something much bigger.

In the week I am writing this, I met a woman at church who had been struggling with loneliness. Her closest friends had moved out of town, and her parents didn't get her desire to follow Christ. The people she'd relied on for relational intimacy had either been taken away or had distanced themselves. So like many in big cities, she found herself surrounded by millions and yet feeling isolated.

Then she said something that I hadn't quite expected. She said, with tears in her eyes, "we've been going through the story of the whole Bible at church, and it's reminded me that God is the answer to my struggle. He is so good to me."

She was not entirely new to Christian things. Yet her understanding of the unswerving faithfulness of God, who sticks with us despite our sin and our struggles, had turned from a flame in her head to a fire in her heart.

More than that, on the roadmap of life she had found the dot that said *You are here* and it made all the difference. It was bringing her more than just comfort. It was bringing contentment. She wasn't merely *enduring* her situation but *enjoying* Jesus as she walked through the difficulties. I was so grateful to God for this reminder that his love really is "better than life" (Psalm 63 v 3), so that his people can praise him whatever their circumstances.

3. Celebrating our situation

or Why singleness is not second best

As I reflected on all that I was learning, I couldn't help wondering where this left me as a single person. The big story of the Bible had taught me that I was wired for relationships. And God had written marriage into the very heart of his big love story. But as a single person, I couldn't help feeling second best—trying to make the most of the "waiting room" stage of life until Mrs Right came along.

Every year of singleness and every engagement announcement in church felt more frustrating than the last. Many in my circle of friends felt the same. Some had never married; others were single again having been widowed or divorced. Yet we all tended to see ourselves like aeroplanes in a holding pattern with the runway obscured from view.

Some single people had been in that holding pattern for a lot longer than me and in some cases confirmed my fears. The things that I felt in embryo they felt in a more fully developed way. I struggled to believe that I could be content as an older single person. My frustrations would just be more intense and scary.

Second best?

To be fair, the Bible's love story *had* helped me make progress in my thinking. Married people display the "earthly" part of God's love story as a husband and wife sacrificially stick with each other. Single people display the "heavenly" part of God's love story by joyfully focusing on their faithful Saviour, as we all will in the new creation.

This should have been good news. My relationship status was an opportunity to enjoy, not an obstacle to overcome. God is a lover who has made us to love like him, and both married and single people reflect his great love story in different ways. But in my experience, being single still felt somehow second best.

So far then, my feelings didn't quite fit the way that the Bible framed things. Singleness isn't God's consolation prize for those who haven't found a spouse: quite the opposite. Jesus, the most confident, contented and cheerful man that has ever lived, never married. But I found it hard to get beyond the fact that I missed out on a physical and emotional intimacy that married people enjoyed, and there was no obvious upside. Surely life would be more fulfilling if I was married.

It took the patient work of several single friends to help me see singleness through God's eyes. In this chapter I want to explore that a little with you. Singleness has real challenges. Yet there are also real opportunities to enjoy. There is a freedom from distraction, and space to enjoy intimacy in many other relationships, and to seek Christ in new ways. But each of these perspectives was hard won.

Enjoying freedom

My first insight came from a young woman who had been "adopted" by a family at church who had young children of their own. From the time they got to know each other, this family had welcomed her into much of their daily life. As a result she was often at their house hanging out socially and enjoying meals with them.

The truth was that "hanging out" often felt more like entering a war zone. There were baby-food landmines underfoot and vomit grenades hurled at unexpected moments. The battle strategy was constantly being revised as children attempted to overthrow parental plans. Tiredness often led to tension. Conversations were snatched and stretched out between the demands of the little people. It was a very different and demanding way of life. The time that the parents had to look beyond their own practical circumstances was drastically reduced.

The apostle Paul says again and again that remaining single means that we can be "undivided" in our devotion to the Lord (1 Corinthians 7 v 28b, 32-35, 38, 39-40): in other words, less distracted from serving God. Of course raising children is one of many ways that God's people can serve God, not a distraction from it. Yet what my friend saw was how its practical demands were often all consuming. It's not that she hated family life, but it taught her not to be quite so envious of it.

This first-hand experience helped her to appreciate the freedom that Paul talks about. The problem for me at the time, was that her description of family life still seemed dreamy, sweet and even attractive. I couldn't quite smell the puke. Now, as a married man, I live her experience out in high definition—including all the unspeakable smells. It's obvious to me now that there is a real freedom in being single.

The "military" life

As a single person, marriage seemed like the promised land—a place of unending ease and comfort. It was easy to forget that marriage would bring its own unique set of burdens. For example, every week my wife and I have to plan in a fairly detailed way where we'll be each day at what time. One of us needs to be around to pick up our kids, prepare food, host guests and balance all kinds of ministry commitments we have between us. To be able to plan for and do these things is a privilege, but the truth is, the need to lock down so much of the week works against my natural inclination—spontaneity. It can feel claustrophobic.

My single friends, on the other hand, can get to the gym on a Saturday morning or go for a run without giving it much thought. If they get a text from a friend, they can be at the pub or even the airport almost at the drop of a hat. More importantly, if someone needs help, they can be available more flexibly. So they can support one another and share Christ with unbelievers in a more spontaneous and reactive kind of way.

Before 8am each day, we have to dress and disciple four people before we leave the house, and then take them to school. Of course we chose these things. To do them is an honour—but it's also exhausting. Some mornings the whole thing can be so stressful that when we reach 8am, we're beating back the tears and we haven't even left the house. Not every marriage looks like ours of course. Not everyone has the commitments that I have or the particular demands of my family. And yet there is no doubt that marriage places a new set of powerful burdens on us.

Contrast that with the morning routine of some of my friends. They ease into the day with a morning playlist; scroll through Instagram to see what's happening in the world; read a book, just for fun; spend time in the Bible— and still have time for a relaxed cup of coffee. Or write a blog. Or just lie in. They are time rich in comparison with us. Time they can spend on themselves and on others.

Now when I actually describe my envious thoughts to my single friends, they often say that they don't recognise this picture at all. I've airbrushed out the very real struggles that they go through too: not least feeling that they have to play "Let's pretend" when it comes to their longings for intimacy. I'm just struck that both marriage and singleness bring their own benefits and burdens—and freedom is one of the differences that the Bible particularly emphasises.

The promises you didn't think you'd have to keep

The freedom we have during seasons of singleness is not just practical but emotional too. Many of the needs that come up in a family are unpredictable and emotionally challenging. In the last few years of my father's life, my mum cared for him largely single-handedly. His movement was very limited. She had to wash him, help him out of bed in the morning and provide for him during the day.

She would routinely ask him what he felt like eating, go out and get the ingredients, cook the food and then find that he didn't feel like eating or couldn't hold it down anyway. She cleaned up his vomit; she drove him to hospital appointments and then rubbed him down afterwards as he struggled with the pain of the journey.

Occasionally, I was involved with a tiny part of what I've just described. I found that even a few hours could feel deeply frustrating. Yet my mum bore this burden day after day after day for years. Being part of this first-hand made me realise something of the scale of what I had signed up for when I stood at the front of church and said:

"To have and to hold, to love and to cherish, for better or for worse, for richer or poorer, till death us do part."

Many couples struggle to imagine anything terrible happening to either of them as they gaze into each others eyes during the wedding service. The reality though is that only God knows what's in store once they walk back down the aisle. My pastor was pretty honest about his own struggles in marriage. I'm so grateful that he crushed the rose-tinted glasses I had when it came to what marriage looked like on the ground. The disciples too seemed to get the seriousness of this commitment when they said: "If this is the situation between a husband and a wife it is better not to marry" (Matthew 19 v 10).

I'm not saying that marriage is worse than singleness. When Jesus' disciples said it was better not to marry, Jesus replied, "There are those who choose to live like eunuchs for the sake of the kingdom of heaven" (Matthew 19 v 12). In other words, because marriage involves such tough responsibilities and commitments, some will choose singleness. Both marriage and singleness have benefits. Both bring burdens. So how do we deal with the pressures of being single in particular?

Enjoying intimacy as a single person

One thing the big story of the Bible helped me get clear was that intimacy is not solely physical; and that it is part of *all* relationships not just marriage. We are wired as God's image-bearers to desire closeness, warmth and affection from others. Although marriage is one very significant way that this can express itself, it's not the only way.

Just think about the intimacy that can be experienced in friendships, families or as part of a crowd watching your country play in a World Cup match for example. So it shouldn't be the case that married people experience intimacy and single people don't. It's part and parcel of all relationships but with varying levels of intensity.

One single friend of mine said recently that marriage seemed to him like "a holy grail of complete otherness"—he could not imagine what the experience of being married would be like. But the reality is that although there are clear differences, relationships outside marriage and inside marriage are not two *entirely different* worlds. They are both part of the relational nature of life that God intended for all of us. There are actually lots of similarities between our relationships with one another and our relationships in marriage.

I'm going to talk more about friendship in chapter five. But two examples that I want to think about here are how we greet each other and what we wear. As relational beings, we desire physical touch from friends and to look attractive on a night out. Although they might be expressed differently, these things are not limited to marriage but part of being made in God's image with relational desires.

Beyond the mistletoe

The New Testament writers expect a certain amount of physicality to our interactions with one another—for everyone in church, not just those who are married. Paul says we should "greet each other with a holy kiss" (Romans 16 v 16) and Peter with "a kiss of love" (1 Peter 5 v 14).

I remember the beginning of a church service a few years ago when a friend of mine, who had been abroad for a little while, came back to church. I knew her well, and it felt appropriate to give her a hug. She confided in me later that although she was content with singleness, the thing she struggled most with was the fact that she rarely got a hug.

She felt guilty about even desiring this. Paul, on the other hand, seems to demand that we find wise, culturally appropriate ways of showing modest physical affection to our brothers and sisters in the church.

There are all kinds of potential pitfalls to this. Paul's words could be abused in an offensive or hypocritical way. I have personally experienced the sense of violation when someone oversteps a boundary. The friend I hugged was someone I knew well, and we were in a public situation open to accountability—at the start of a church service.

One of the things that surprised me about Paul's instruction about physical greetings is that he even gave it to the Corinthian church. This community was rife with sexual promiscuity. If there was one place to be cautious, it was there. Yet it seems that the principle was too important to ignore. It could be a hand on a shoulder, a fist pump, a warm handshake, a friendly hug, in some cultures a kiss—a touch that publicly acknowledges our bond with other members of Christ's body.

Growing up, I would sometimes find myself in church services in which the vicar would announce that it was time to share "the sign of peace". People got out of their seats to shake hands with those around them. I dreaded it. Now I look forward to it. It feels like a fitting way of greeting "all God's people" with an appropriate physical sign of affection, without slipping into another danger: that of showing favouritism (1 Thessalonians 5 v 26).

Grey isn't always fashionable

Another way that we live out our relational connectedness is in what we wear. 1 Timothy 2 v 8-10 warns us against investing too much time, expense, and effort when it comes to our appearance. However, it reminds us too that we should not go around naked but dress ourselves in a way that is fitting.

Although this passage is focused on women, it is part of a section applying a more general principle about the way both sexes can honour God. While it may have been particularly pressing to address women in that context, the issue of appropriateness in our dress is not limited to either sex. I don't think I should show up at church naked either. Especially not if I'm preaching.

In the same way that exercise and keeping our bodies in shape is of "some value" (1 Timothy 4 v 8) and a way of honouring God's creation, so it is of some value to dress with care and make an effort to look nice. We just do that in a way that recognises that these things are not ultimate.

The book of Proverbs hints at both sides of this in its final chapter. It describes a woman of "noble" character. She is meant to be an idealised example for women to follow. She takes care over her appearance—"clothed in fine linen and purple" (Proverbs 31 v 22)—and is marked out by her spiritual appearance too—"clothed in strength and dignity" (v 25). In other words, she doesn't neglect her appearance *or* make her appearance the main thing.

Enjoying Christ

So far I've described how my friends taught me to enjoy the freedom that singleness gave me to serve God and to enjoy the everyday intimacy of interacting with friends and family. One more friend, though, pointed me to how I could actually channel my struggles into enjoying Jesus.

I mentioned earlier that the love we crave is a signpost to something more—the God of love himself. C.S. Lewis, a Christian author that I have come to love, gets really practical with this. He talks about following or "looking along" our desires back to the source.

He describes a day when he saw a single beam of light break into his dark shed. It looked beautiful as he stared at it, watching the light and the dust dance around. But then, instead of looking at it, he moved position to look *along* the beam of light. Suddenly a much bigger world opened up that tracked back to the sun itself. When it comes to relationships, the best moments are a shadow of something better: of divine reality.

How not to stare

Another friend taught me to use of this principle when struggling with lust. He had learnt to "look along" his desires to the God they point to. Some years ago the Royal Academy ran an exhibition called "Modigliani and his models". Some of it was made up of nude portraits, and reproductions were plastered all over London Underground tube stations as part of the publicity campaign. My friend was struggling with this as he travelled around. He found himself caught between lustful staring and shameful avoidance. He felt that he had to play "Let's pretend" with his sexuality.

One day something changed. Stepping off a tube train, he found himself confronted by yet another one of these posters, as he often did. Only this time, his response was different. For the first time, he found himself able to say in his heart "Praise God for this woman's beauty".

He didn't need to avoid the obvious beauty of the model. Neither did he find himself drawn into lust. Instead he acknowledged his desire and followed it to its source— to God himself. His desire was a signpost to the stars. In other words, it connected him to his creator.

As I thought about it, I remember thinking that he could have gone even further. It isn't just God's goodness in making us that we can praise, but his goodness in saving us too. The spark my friend felt when he looked at that woman was a faint glimpse of the affection that Christ offers us.

My friend taught me that while restraint is good, rejoicing

is better. It is good to look elsewhere when our gaze tempts us to sin. How much better, though, if that very moment becomes an opportunity to rejoice in Jesus and laugh in the face of the tempter (Psalm 37 v 12-13). Countless books wisely tell us to train our eyes to look elsewhere. The real issue though is to train our eyes to "look along" our desire to Christ.

This is not just for single people! In marriage it has been a huge encouragement too, because sex and relationships are often not what the James Bond movies and the romantic comedies teach us to expect. In place of the multiple mutual orgasms of the big screen there is often discomfort, boredom, tiredness and embarrassment about our bodies. All this gets in the way of the mountain-top experience that we crave. And even when it kind of works out, it's over too soon.

I remember an evening recently when I had been teaching on how God had wired us to enjoy relationships. I got home and pretty much immediately had a massive argument with my wife. I sat at the dining-room table, got out my laptop and began to work, while she sat at the other end doing her own jobs. We didn't speak for an hour. Then she went to bed without saying a word, and I made no effort to stop her.

Mercifully she didn't leave me for good—just the room. Yet at painful times like these I find myself turning to the Lord and remembering verses like "Never will I leave you; never will I forsake you" (Hebrews 13 v 5) and "Though my father and mother forsake me, the LORD will receive me" (Psalm 27 v 10).

For me, when intimacy works, I can "look along" it to something much better: a much richer intensity of communion with Jesus. But in the many times when all kinds of obstacles get in the way of the experience I crave, I can recognise that there is forgiveness for my failure, and something that is ultimately more lasting and profound in my relationship with Christ.

Everyone's situation is different, whether married or single. And yet the reality is that both are hard. The comfort of Christ can sustain us both. I don't want to be glib or pretend that what I've described made all the struggles disappear. It didn't. But it did give me a positive way of looking at things that didn't mean denying my desires or taking my eyes off Christ. I could enjoy my freedom to serve Christ without distraction. I could enjoy the intimacy that the relationships in my church community made possible. Even the times when I was struggling to be content, were an opportunity to remember the sweetness of my Saviour.

My situation has changed. I am no longer single. But many of my single Christian friends, both straight and same-sex attracted, testify to the sustaining power of these truths. Marriage brings its own challenges. We'll touch on these in the next two chapters.

4. Faithful

or Why anniversaries matter more than weddings

When I was about twelve, I remember being dragged along to my grandparents' wedding-anniversary celebration. They renewed their vows, ate like kings and stared tenderly into each other's eyes. Back then, a party with the extended family felt more like a pain than a pleasure. But I've come to realise that wedding anniversaries are actually wonderful celebrations of faithful love. For Christians, the commitment that they represent is an essential part of putting God's passionate, faithful and life-giving love on display.

In fact a wedding anniversary actually pictures God's love far better than "the big day". It reflects something more profound than the passion of young love—the perseverance of faithful commitment.

The blog that blew up my view of marriage

It was another anniversary story that helped me to see this clearly—the story of bloggers Ian and Larissa Murphy. I stumbled across a blog post where they were writing with passion about their tenth year together. But this had been no ordinary ten years. Just before these university sweethearts were married, Ian suffered a traumatic brain injury leaving him severely disabled. He had been on his way to work to earn money for an engagement ring, when his car slammed into a jeep. Their plans and dreams were shattered, but their love wasn't. Larissa wrote:

Ten years ago we were burning with wanting and with love that laid on the surface of everything we touched. Ten years has dug that love deeper, so deep that sometimes it can't even be found on the surface, but it's there because we promised it always would be ...

Thank you, after ten years, for always choosing love, always choosing forgiveness, always choosing me. Even in my darkest, not unlike today, you hem me in and anchor my heart and never feed me guilt.

Thank you for not giving up—on me, this marriage or this life-long attempt at understanding him.

I love you, my tom cruise.[1]

---

1   ianandlarissa.com/ten (Accessed 21st March 2018)

It was hard not to be amazed by their committed, faithful love. It was a far cry from the selfishness that I often bring into my own marriage.

For example, a few years ago my wife and I were thinking through how we could serve each other better in our marriage. As we chatted, she mentioned one of the things that she was finding hard. It was the time that I got home in the evenings. I often arrived home later than the time that I had said I would that day. As is often the case, it's the small things that end up becoming big frustrations.

Now, there were times when the reason for this was unavoidable. Transport problems, a meeting that overran or an unexpected conversation late in the day. But the truth was that a lot of the time this was not the case. The reason was that I simply lost track of time. After this chat I confessed, prayed and promised to do better. And yet to this day I still struggle. Again, while this might seem a small thing, it's symptomatic of something bigger. When the Michelins hit the highway, my attitude to my spouse can be dramatically self-centred, as if she were there merely to meet my needs on my terms at my convenience.

The story of Ian and Larissa has encouraged me to think through again how God's big picture for marriage works out at ground level. They have been very open about what has sustained their marriage. For them it comes down to knowing its purpose. Knowing something's purpose makes all the difference.

To take a trivial example, when my four-year-old daughter tries to eat soup with a knife, she quickly gets frustrated. I need to tell her that she's misunderstood the purpose of a knife. If she carries on, she'll not only be frustrated but might get hurt. In a similar way, if we misunderstand the purpose of marriage we can end up going about it in a way that frustrates us and leaves us hurt. If marriage was just about carefree sexual gratification, there would have been no future for Ian and Larissa after Ian's accident—only frustration and hurt. But the Bible's vision is much grander than that.

Why sex isn't at the centre

It turns out that the purpose of marriage is not about serving ourselves but serving God. The very first marriage in the Bible was about serving God in the work of subduing the earth (Genesis 1 v 28). So you could say that sex comes with a price tag labelled "service". Of course service is part of being a Christian whether we're married or single. The danger we face is thinking of marriage as a kind of break clause in the Christian life, when service stops and sex begins. This might not be the thought in the front of our minds. Our culture, however, is constantly drip-feeding us the idea that a sexual relationship is mainly focused on whatever pleases *you*. In fact it's an opportunity to serve God together in a new way.

What does the service God desires from married couples look like? The thrust of the Bible seems to be that the love they experience should overflow to others. We see this pattern of overflowing love play out throughout the story of the Bible. For example, even when God pledges himself to a particular group of people, it is for the sake of blessing the world. He says to Abraham, "All peoples on earth will be blessed through you" (Genesis 12 v 1). In other words, God's love to us is always meant to overflow to others.

When it comes to the gift of marriage, the love of the man and woman is not meant to turn in on itself but to move towards others. I was struck to discover that in the Song of Songs, the most personal love poem in the Bible, we see a glimpse of this in picture language too. It's imagery is full of the excitement of personal devotion in the springtime, a time of waiting for fruit to ripen (2 v 10-13). However, it also looks forward to a time of very public fruitfulness (7 v 12) when the vines bud and their blossoms open and pomegranates bloom. Personal intimacy overflows into public fruitfulness.

One couple I know model this constantly. When they go on holiday, they seem to make a point of asking, "Who can we visit in that area to encourage while we're there?" It is rare to be invited to their house and find that they are not hosting a missionary family or mentoring a young friend. Having children is seen as an opportunity to widen their networks, not close them down.

Now, they have a particular set of gifts and capacities. We praise God for them, but mostly we feel exhausted just watching them! My wife and I would burn out trying to match what this couple seem to do effortlessly. But the attitude behind it seems to capture God's heart. It's a relational generosity that pushes back on a "because I'm worth it" culture that prizes looking after number one.

I've tried to break down the things that their lifestyle seems to manifest. They flow from the Bible's full-orbed picture of what marriage involves. And it's clearly more than a private relationship centred around sex. It's the place for procreation, a picture of the faithful love of God, an opportunity to proclaim that love in Christ and a place for many to experience that love in community.

The place for procreation

Sex within heterosexual marriage by its very nature is open to the creation of new life. In this way married couples physically image God's life-giving love. In fact the first man and woman were called to "be fruitful and multiply; fill the earth and subdue it" (Genesis 1 v 28). This meant that they were put together for a bigger purpose than sex: to fill the earth with faithful image-bearers who would care for it.

Of course not every marriage can bear children. Infertility is a problem that affects about one in six couples today. I know many who have struggled personally with this—it can be a heartbreaking and deeply traumatic experience. In the Bible childlessness causes much mourning and anguished prayer (for example, Hannah in 1 Samuel 1). God acknowledges the sadness it causes as one of the painful realities of living in a broken world. Childless couples should in no way feel guilty about struggling with it. They very much need the support and prayers of friends around them. Again, there are all kinds of other situations in which children are wonderfully raised, such as by adoption or fostering. While these things are not always straightforward, it does seem clear that marriage is the environment in which God intends children to be ordinarily conceived and nurtured (Genesis 1 v 27-28; 2 v 24). In line with this, social science seems to consistently show that "children who are raised by their married, biological parents enjoy better physical, cognitive and emotional outcomes, on average, than children who are raised in other circumstances."[2]

An opportunity for proclamation

Marriage also creates new opportunities for evangelism. While the first man and woman were tasked with biological reproduction, we are now tasked with spiritual reproduction as well. We do this not only by nurturing children in the faith but by sharing the gospel with unbelievers.

In fact in the book of Colossians, the apostle Paul seems to deliberately mirror the language of Genesis 1 v 28 in order to explain this. He shows that faithful image bearers today are not the biological offspring of believers but their spiritual offspring. It is those who have understood God's grace in the gospel:

---

2   https://bit.ly/2PCNN3E (Accessed 1st May 2019)

The gospel is bearing fruit and growing throughout the whole world—just as it has been doing among you since the day you heard it and truly understood God's grace.
(Colossians 1 v 6)

It's been a privilege as a couple to learn from others who model this. We've watched many open up their doors for hospitality with their neighbours, host events around Christmas time for local residents, and use children's parties as a chance for church family to meet non-Christian friends. We've found it a healthy challenge to ask ourselves, "How are we using our marriage to proclaim Christ?"

A picture of faithfulness

I always find it sobering to remember that our faithfulness to one another points out what God is like to a watching world. Once again, we are image-bearers putting God on display. Sure, no one has ever blatantly pointed out the link: "Aha, because you are faithful to your spouse I now realise that God is faithful". Even so, I find that people are quick to notice when we slip up if we are public about our faith. As a result, sometimes God gets written off because of our actions.

People notice whether what we say matches what we do. Like it or not, they read about our Lord off the pages of our lives. They assume we'll bear the family likeness.

This is a great opportunity for us to speak to the world as God's image-bearers. For example, in a society where living together is more common than marriage, simply bothering to publicly declare our commitment to one another is unusual. As relationship breakups become increasingly common, faithful marriage becomes oddly prominent. So even when the fire feels cold, we try to remember that as God's image bearers, we are committed to putting his faithfulness on display. I really don't want to pretend that this is always easy. It certainly hasn't been for Ian and Larissa. But it is part of the calling of marriage.

A place of welcome

I mentioned earlier a couple who have modelled relational generosity in their marriage when on holiday and when friends visit. They do it with their local community too. You could call it seeking to live with "porous boundaries". Their home is a special place for the family and yet often open to visitors. We've known the temptation as a married couple to lock the doors and just look inward, when the Bible repeatedly encourages all Christians to look outward. One reason we should keep the fire burning inside is so that we can warm others outside.

Showing hospitality is one key way that we can do this (Romans 12 v 3; Hebrews 13 v 2; 1 Peter 4 v 9). We've found that welcoming strangers into family life widens our circle of love and affection, and has allowed others to support us when life has been tough. It has also helped all of us to grow in godliness as we have journeyed with people who are different from us.

Examples that have inspired us include friends who have used their home to host international students as lodgers or vulnerable people in need of refuge; others who regularly use their home as a place to read the Bible and pray with local people; those who have asked the same person to babysit a number of times in order to mentor and encourage them; couples who have fostered children; and friends who have deliberately chosen for a time to live with another couple in a community house.

Our circumstances and giftings will be different. But it is the attitude behind these examples rather than precisely how they work out that is key. So it's worth thinking creatively about opportunities where you are to open the borders of your home in life-giving ways.

Supporting faithfulness

What Ian and Larissa are doing would be impossible to do alone. They speak often of how it is only because of the love and support of others that they are able to keep going. Engagement courses and marriage preparation classes have really helped me personally and many others in the churches I have served in—they ground couples in the Bible's big story as well as the nitty-gritty details. Marriage refreshers, parenting courses and toddler groups have also encouraged us as a young family and connected us to others.

It's not so much the "course" that matters, though, but the culture: a culture that says it's okay to be honest about our struggles. One of the very sad realities of being a pastor is being faced with how often problems in a marriage only seem to surface when things are almost irreconcilable. And like the example I shared from my own life, things often seem to fall apart in the everyday unacknowledged struggles, rather than dramatic calamitous failures.

Having access to marriage counselling, and removing any stigma that might be attached to using it, might be another step in the right direction. But I wonder if we need to work hard to provide safe spaces where couples, or individual spouses in same-sex prayer groups can have gracious but frank discussions with each other about how their relationships are going. No one should feel isolated. Real openness is always tough; it will take courage for couples to begin to model this in church life, but it's vital.

Tragically, in a fallen world, fallen men and women have fallen marriages. We might strive to live according to the wonderful vision of what marriage really is in God's design, but we will always fall short. Sometimes badly. Although we are called to be faithful, I would never counsel anyone to remain in a marriage that is abusive. If that is you, can I urge you to seek help immediately.

Where faithfulness leads

Finally, I need to be constantly reminded of the end of the story—the wedding supper of the Lamb:

Then I saw a new heaven and a new earth, for the first heaven and the first earth had passed away, and there was no longer any sea. I saw the Holy City, the new Jerusalem, coming down out of heaven from God, prepared as a bride beautifully dressed for her husband. And I heard a loud voice from the throne saying, 'Look! God's dwelling-place is now among the people, and he will dwell with them. They will be his people, and God himself will be with them and be their God. "He will wipe every tear from their eyes. There will be no more death" or mourning or crying or pain, for the old order of things has passed away. (Revelation 21 v 1-4)

This is a sumptuous future hope—food and intimacy, the ultimate marriage and supper! The descriptions are dazzling: shining like crystal, overwhelmed with comfort, communing with Christ. We're all invited. Those who respond will all get to enjoy it. And in this brief moment before the Bridegroom comes, we can testify to this ultimate marriage.

Whether we happen to be married or single, we all wrestle with temptation, selfishness and shame. These verses are a huge encouragement to me and many friends, both married and single, to battle together as the bride of Christ and witness to his good news for the world.

5. Friendship

or Why "the one" isn't enough

I have had the privilege of having a close lifelong friend. He's the kind of guy who keeps cropping up in the photo albums. He's been through pretty much everything with me. He's seen me at my worst with my head over the toilet seat. He's encouraged me to be my best.

When I got my first real job *and* when the interviews were a nightmare, he was there. When I needed someone to get me through bad relationship breakups—he was my go-to guy. The first number I dialled when I thought I'd found "the one" was his. He knows more about me than I'd like to admit. We've fought together, laughed together and mourned together.

When children came along, he got in his car to come and visit. In many of the big moments of my life, he's been close by. That kind of friendship is a special thing and has brought real joy and depth to my life. The Bible reminds us that our closest friendships should do just that:

> *Perfume and incense bring joy to the heart, and the pleasantness of a friend springs from their heartfelt advice.*   *(Proverbs 27 v 9)*

The ancient custom of pouring perfume on a guest would have been very welcome in the Mediterranean heat and dust. In the same way, when a friend shares their life and wisdom, it is a great source of joy.

Right person, wrong expectations

When I stood at the altar looking into my wife-to-be's eyes, I actually believed that she would complete me in every way. Admirably optimistic but woefully unrealistic! My wife can't possibly bear the weight of all my relational needs. Nor I hers. No one person, let alone a sinful person, can do that. To be my counsellor, lover, wisdom giver and shoulder to cry on in all areas of my life, all the time, is too much to expect of anyone.

So when it comes to remaining faithfully committed to my spouse, I actually need a network of people. It makes sense that Paul wrote Ephesians 4 (about relationships in the church) before Ephesians 5 (relationships in marriage). Our wider network supports the narrower ones. My single friends would say exactly the same thing about imaging God faithfully in their situation. In order to remain faithfully committed to Christ, they need a network of people around them.

The friend I described earlier is also a Christian. I'm very blessed that we grew up together and then both came to faith at similar points in adult life. We found ourselves walking out into a world where most people didn't share our new way of seeing it. For us, there was the same sense of anticipation that you have when a new government has won by a landslide. We were part of a new wave of change. The issue was that many of our friends seemed to have missed the news.

On the one hand, it was tempting to assimilate—just to fit in with the indifference that many of our friends had towards religion. On the other hand, it was easy to resort to isolation: to adopt a bunker mentality that tried to avoid conflict and wait until culture turned a corner. The problem was that the corner was never going to come. Both temptations meant that there were some moments when life could become very lonely.

I was so grateful to be able to bounce ideas off my friend, pray with him, and have him rein me in when I decided to do something stupid. Like Paul and Timothy, we not only shared history but values too (2 Timothy 3 v 10-11). I had many good friends who were not Christians. And yet I couldn't get away from the fact that my belief in Jesus began to shape everything I did in profound ways. This meant my *best* friends became those that pointed me away from sin and towards my Saviour. So there has been a joy in having friends whose foundational way of looking at the world aligns with mine.

Reality bites

Being brutally honest, I have also been let down by friends too. Whenever you make yourself vulnerable, you open yourself up to hurt. I remember once going round to a friend's flat (let's call him Jeff) to vent. I was frustrated with another friend (who I'll call Mike), who had bailed out of a commitment at the last minute. He seemed to be making a habit of messing me around.

The next day, having calmed down a bit, it was clear to me that I'd overreacted. It was a wrong that I should have overlooked. But by then Jeff had taken it upon himself to fill Mike in. Once it was out in the open, far more damage was done to our whole friendship group than was necessary. I was bruised, and it took time for us to trust each other again.

There is a fee to pay for friendship: the prospect of pain. It was one of those stark reminders, that we need to have realistic expectations, even of close friends. Having said all this, the risks are worth it. We need friendships.

My friendship formula

I've found it helpful to think about my relationships in three categories: The first are *comrades*. These are people I share goals with. For example, my work colleagues, gym buddies, the school-run crowd or the neighbours I tag team with when our cars need repairing. I need these relationships. Life wouldn't function without them. But when my goals change because I move jobs or flat, it's easy to lose touch with comrades.

Then there's **kin**. These are the family and friends who I know will be there if I need them. I can go for a long time without seeing them, but when we meet, we basically pick up where we left off. In a crisis they'll pull out all the stops to help out. We understand that we have a duty of care for each other, however emotionally connected we happen to feel at the time.

Finally, there are **confidantes**. I guess this is what I was describing with my friend at the beginning. He's someone I can share *everything* with and open up to, and who has stuck with me throughout my life. I think this is what the writer of Proverbs is talking about when he says, "One who has unreliable friends soon comes to ruin, but there is a friend who sticks closer than a brother" (Proverbs 18 v 24). Jesus seemed to care about confidantes too. He clearly had particularly close relationships with people like Peter, James and John, and with Lazarus, Mary and Martha.

It's difficult to sustain the confidante-type relationship nowadays for all kinds of reasons. For example, I've got hundreds of Facebook "friends" who get very little of my attention. Frankly, that probably warps my view of friendship a little. It's a far cry from the Bible's vision of face-to-face encounters (e.g. Exodus 33 v 11). In fact the apostle John even stops his correspondence short because he would rather speak in person:

I have much to write to you, but I do not want to use paper and ink. Instead, I hope to visit you and talk with you face to face, so that our joy may be complete.

(2 John 1 v 12)

John is saying, in effect, *although I could write more down in this letter, there is something so valuable about face-to-face contact that I'm going to hold back until I see you.* The trouble is, face-to-face contact is increasingly difficult to achieve. Because we are so mobile, being in the right place at the right time to meet people is harder work than it once was.

There are other factors at play too. When I've travelled to other parts of the world, the blind spots of my own culture have always become a lot clearer. I breathe the air of individualism here in the UK. I wonder whether I can overvalue personal comfort and private space, which means I find it harder to let people into the little time and space that I do have. It's easy for me, without realising it, to subtly isolate myself from people.

Life circumstances can also be pretty transient—especially in large cities. I spoke to a friend just recently who was thinking of moving out of London because as quickly as he made meaningful friendships, they moved on, leaving him back at square one.

Tips for the treasure hunt

So far, then, we've seen that we should treasure confidantes, but they are hard to come by. How can we cultivate these relationships? Here are some suggestions that have helped me along the way:

Explore your church

I can safely say that some of the most precious moments of my life have been caught up with the love, hospitality and care of my church family. Don't misunderstand me though. That doesn't mean that church friendships are always easy. There is no doubt that sometimes investing in relationships, even in church, means that we open ourselves up to get hurt. But it is worth it.

For me the hardest part was the decision to make going to church more than just an event I attended. When it was just an event, I could slip in five minutes after the start of the service and sneak off during the final song, and feel quite satisfied. I'd "done" church.

If I was going to be part of the community, I had to do church differently—on Sundays and throughout the week. I began to hang around to help clear up. I signed up to a fellowship group and actually showed up. It was painful at first. I felt awkward and exposed. However, I was welcomed, and in time those relationships matured. Stick with the church: whether you are investigating it, reconnecting with it, or persevering as a long-serving member. It's hard to be loved if you are not there.

Evaluate your commitment

Friendship takes effort. Emotionally, we have to let people into our mess. Practically, if we're serious about developing friendships, we've got to be prepared to spend time with people. For me, that means being prepared to block out time in the diary and being prepared to travel.

It means regularly serving alongside people at church. It also means resisting my urge to move to a new area or ministry, so that I can invest in people locally.

I think of people who planned to be in the neighbourhood so that we could meet up week by week. It took effort! We have found that having committed to be godparents helps us to be intentional about meeting up with friends who have moved away. We want to be realistic of course, but we also want to take the public commitment we made to support them and their children seriously.

Embrace groups

A good friend of mine said recently that *intimacy* doesn't have to mean *exclusivity*. It doesn't have to be one to one. It's a great point. Living in a shared flat or being part of a church community group that really "do life" together can be an incredibly intimate thing.

I've had the privilege for the last few years of being part of a community church that feels like this. Despite the highly mobile nature of London life, many have committed to remaining part of the church for several years. The result is that visitors say that visiting it feels like being welcomed into a family. That's what it feels like to me too. Those relationships are precious.

Establish others

Among my single friends, one of the ongoing struggles for some has been not being able to nurture children. Both male and female friends have chatted about how this can be a painful yearning—even when otherwise they feel content with being single. Thinking about what some have called "spiritual parenting" can help. We nurture spiritual children when we help to establish them in their faith through wise counsel, Bible-reading and prayer.

Recently, one of my friends was asked out of the blue to be a "spiritual mum". She found it an honour to be asked. It had looked as if biological or adopted children might not be part of God's plan for her life. The chance to nurture a younger woman in this way proved to be a real blessing in her life.

Experiment

The truth is that we can only sustain a tiny number of confidante-type friendships. We are blessed to have even one! But if we *are* looking to develop them, trying new things might help if other existing ways of growing friendships are proving difficult. It's always easier to build up relationships when you are working together on a project like playing sport or clearing the gutters.

Some that I know have intentionally chosen to live in a community house with others, with the aim of building deep friendships. In other words, we might need to be creative.

There is a certain mystery, though, around which friendships work and which don't. So we need patience. The friendships I enjoy now didn't develop overnight. They matured through the ups and downs of both the mundane and the major events in my life. All of this takes time and trust in God's good plans for us.

Enlarge your faith

I was encouraged by one pastor who wrote that we shouldn't just focus on how to *find* good friends but also on how to *be* a good friend. Being a good friend means being able to give good advice. Remember that "perfume and incense bring joy to the heart, and the pleasantness of a friend springs from their heartfelt advice" (Proverbs 27 v 9). This means seeking to grow in our knowledge of the wisdom in God's word. One of my friends can make me belly laugh and banter with the best of them. But I never leave his company without him sharing something that he's been humbled by in God's word. He's a friend I cherish. It's an old saying, but it is true: *To get a friend, you need to be a friend.*

Experience Christ

Despite our best efforts, our friends will still let us down and can't always be there for us. Having good, close friends will not fix all your problems. But there is one friend who has always been there for me, who *has* been able to stick closer than a brother. His name is Jesus.

The truth is, there are times, even as a married person, when we can feel intensely lonely. It's a surreal and scary experience to share the same space as someone and yet feel as if you're on a different planet. Yet most people will testify to having experienced this. The comfort we need at times like those comes from Christ. No one gets closer than the One who promises to be in us and that we are in him (1 John 4 v 15-16).

This last point is so important: because as much as we've talked about gaining friends, as we seek to love as God loves, when it comes to sexuality, we may also lose friends too. A friend of mine is same-sex attracted and passionate about God's vision for his life of faithful celibacy. He's spoken about how it is Christ and his promises that sustain him. Mark 10 v 28-30 has been particularly precious to him:

"Truly I tell you," Jesus replied, "no one who has left home or brothers or sisters or mother or father or children or fields for me and the gospel will fail to receive a hundred times as much in this present age: homes, brothers, sisters, mothers, children and fields—along with persecutions—and in the age to come eternal life."

In the end, Jesus seems to be saying this: *I promise to work for you and be with you in such a way that in the end you will not be able to say that you have sacrificed anything.*

One thing that has struck me as I've reflected on these words is that just before Jesus said them, a rich man had given up following him because the cost seemed too high. He was asked whether he would choose Jesus or lifestyle as most precious in his life. He chose lifestyle. But Jesus says that there is no lifestyle choice we could make that would be better than following him and his words. He will not short-change us—now or ever. When we see him face to face, we will wonder how we ever could have doubted that following him would be worth it.

Food for the journey

It is promises like these that sustain my friend and that sustain us. As I've prepared this material I've spoken to many people who are making very hard sacrifices in the kind of culture we live in. Whether single, divorced, same-sex attracted and celibate, or those struggling in tough marriages, I've heard the same testimony again and again. They persevere by the sustaining power of Jesus in the present. They push on for the promises of supernatural satisfaction he has made about the future.

We've thought about how the Christian community can support us as we seek to love as God loves. How though do we speak to those around us who don't share our views? We'll think about this in our final chapter.

6. Speaking to our world

or Why "Stop it!" just won't do

This book has been a very personal journey. My hope is that there might be ways in which you see how your journey connects with it. Of course we all have stories that are very different in the details. However, we share in the struggle of working out just what it means to love and be loved.

The big story of the Bible has taught me that at the heart of that struggle is the realisation that we are all made in God's image—a lover who made us to love like he loves. I've tried to map out the journey of discovery that I've been on, as this love story began to make sense of my experiences.

But if this love story is true, it has implications for how we interact with the watching world. How do we communicate this to a culture that often does not agree with it? How do we live it out when those around us simply don't start with the same assumptions that we hold dear? The main focus of this book hasn't been to address this. But I want to finish by giving some pointers.

Common ground

One thing I'm constantly finding is that we actually have a lot in common with those sceptical of Christianity as we come to this conversation. We all want to be happy. We all want to flourish by being the people that we believe we truly are. However, at the core of our faith is the belief that God has not left us to guess the answers to these central questions of our existence. As we embrace God's design, we increasingly experience that it works for us and for our world.

The subject of sexuality and our hunger for intimacy should be a way into talking about our faith rather than something that Christians run away from. Some friends of mine, Glen Scrivener and Glynn Harrison, came up with four expressions that have helped me to bring the Christian perspective on sex into conversations with grace and truth: "thank you", "sorry", "please" and "never".[3]

1. Thank you

The cultural shift over the last few decades known as the sexual revolution has been a wake-up call for Christians across the West. It has challenged and provoked us. It

---

3 Glen came up with "thank you, sorry, please" as a summary of some of the ideas in *A Better Story* and Glynn added "never" later.

has exposed our fear and shame. It has shone a light on our hypocrisy and abuse and cover-up in our churches. Sometimes, too, those seeking to promote these secular ideals have modelled compassion and sensitivity when we have shown prejudice and bigotry.

We disagree profoundly with our society's view of human nature, and fear where it's all heading. But that shouldn't stop us being grateful for the way it has challenged us. Even though we may disagree with its answers, the sexual revolution poses some great questions. Let's acknowledge that. So before we get on to our differences let's start with what we have in common. And where the revolution has sent us back to our Bibles to discover what it really says about sex, let's be prepared to say "thank you".

And mean it.

I've discovered that God is a lover, who made us to love like him—passionate, faithful and life-giving. He invented sex—but sometimes in speaking to Christians, you wouldn't know it. In fact sometimes, to the outsider looking in, it can seem that sex is an embarrassment to Christians far more than a blessing. It's as if God created our head, legs and arms, but the devil slapped on our genitals.[4]

Dig into the text of the Bible, though, and you uncover a book that embraces the reality of sensual, physical longing in human sexuality. Think for example of the *Song of Songs*:

---

4   See Glynn Harrison's book *A Better Story*, Chapter 7—"The Casualties of
    the Revolution—Double jeopardy of shame".

> *"Let him kiss me with the kisses of his mouth! For your*
> *love is better than wine, your anointing oils are fragrant,*
> *your name is perfume poured out. ... How beautiful are*
> *you, my love, how very beautiful. ... Your hair is like a*
> *flock of goats moving down the slopes of Gilead ... your*
> *lips are like a crimson thread and your mouth is lovely. ...*
> *Your two breasts are like two fawns, twins of a gazelle."*
> *(Song of Songs 1 v 1-2; 4 v 1, 3, 5)*

Why put such turbo-charged erotic material in the middle of the Old Testament? Partly because the writer wants to be real about the intensity of our God-given sexual feelings. So we want to express our gratitude—to say "thank you"—for some of the effects of the sexual revolution. It has brought into fresh focus the biblical idea that sex is to be enjoyed and honoured as part of what it means to be made in the image of God. Part of celebrating his passionate, fruitful and life-giving love.

It's worth saying that the Bible's joyful affirmation of sex doesn't mean a celebration of promiscuity. The intimate love of the couple in *Song of Songs* is fenced in for marriage (2 v 7; 3 v 5; 8 v 4). This means that there must also be an appropriate modesty when it comes to sex.

It also doesn't mean that we'll find that physical intimacy comes easily. As we saw earlier, when God originally created the first man and woman, they enjoyed a shamelessness with one another and felt no need to cover up. But when they rebelled against God, they lost trust in God and each other which made it hard for them to be open. We inherit this and can find it hard to be fully open about our most intimate thoughts and feelings in front of one another.

When I meet with friends who ask me about my views on sex, I start by saying that I'm grateful for the age we live in. It has reminded the church of what has sometimes been obscured: sex is a divine gift from a God who is, at his core, a lover.

2. Sorry

We need to admit that sometimes the way Christians have spoken about these issues has been deeply unhelpful. I recently heard the story of a woman called Michelle. She was a 28-year-old full-time student who was unmarried and pregnant. She felt alone, afraid and ashamed. And the tragedy was this: she was "convinced her church family would shun her".[5] She felt forced to give up her child.

The attitude that Michelle faced was not only un-Christian but made a difficult situation even worse. Now, let's be clear: the default attitude of every Christian today is *not* harsh judgmentalism. Even Michelle's fears could have been based on false assumptions about how her family would react. But it is true to say that harsh judgmentalism and misunderstanding are more common than they should be.

These misunderstandings can be seen down the centuries too. There have been times when the way that Christians

---

5 Bob Smietana, "Single Mothers, Second Chances", https://bit.ly/2Tp0PCm (Acccessed 1st May 2019).

have handled truth has been heavy handed and unloving. In the early nineteenth century, homes for "fallen women" and unwed mothers were set up. They would hide their names to maintain the honour of their families. They aimed to seclude the women from sin so that in time they could be integrated back into society.[6] In other words, the consequences of sex outside marriage led to the shaming and seclusion of women.

Another area of failure can be the deeply inconsistent approach to divorce in some churches. Despite the stated high view of marriage, some churches have a very relaxed approach to divorce while being very tough on, for example, same-sex attraction. One is treated as "just one of those things"; the other is a key topic for discipleship. So church seminars on sexual orientation might proliferate but those on divorce seem infrequent and apologetic.

This is, of course, a generalisation. There are times when divorce is the tragic course of action that clearly has to be taken. Struggles with sexual orientation and struggles in marriage need to be treated with great care. Individual circumstances need to be considered in each case. Yet often it appears as if we are applying a double standard in how we treat people. For this we need to say sorry.

Sometimes churches have not made it easy to live as a single person. This has made it harder for many to live out God's vision for human flourishing. Single people

---

6   https://nyti.ms/2TYjs4k (Accessed 1st May 2019).

in their thirties or beyond have sadly sometimes been considered odd. Pressure is put on kids to get married. Sermon illustrations can focus heavily on family life. Well-meaning friends can try to matchmake without really knowing what people are going through or what they actually want. Community life can seem to revolve around families in an exclusive way.

Such churches might say that singleness is special. Yet it can be hard not to feel that they are somehow "substandard", whether straight, same-sex attracted or still working out their sexuality. This is yet another area where the church needs to grow.

But perhaps most awful of all are the revelations of abuse among Christian leaders. Those who have claimed to speak for the vulnerable have been involved in abusing them. Quite simply, they have disgraced the name of Christ.

Where we, the church, have acted un-Christianly, we need to say sorry. *God is a lover who made us to love like him*—in passionate, faithful and life giving ways. The examples I have shared above are anything but that.

At the beginning of the service in my church we have these words displayed on screen: "No perfect people allowed". It's a reminder to everyone present that Christians don't claim to be morally sorted. We are on a journey of repentance and faith, and we welcome all who turn up. Often we make mistakes. It's not just church leaders that bear the blame and the responsibility to put things right, but everyone who calls themselves a follower of Christ.

Just recently I was speaking to a friend who is not a Christian believer, and explained to him that I was writing this book. He began to shift nervously from side to side. It's a sign I've come to recognise as someone preparing themselves to make a quick exit. But the mood changed when I said I thought that Christians need to say sorry for some of the ways we expressed things. I hadn't changed my mind about the fundamentals, but I needed to admit that I had been thoughtless and unloving in how I had spoken about these issues.

It completely changed the conversation. We ended up chatting about the Christian view of sexuality for about an hour. Too often I've come across as "holier than thou" and for that I need to say sorry and repent.

3. Please

Next, we—followers of Jesus—need to ask our society to let us tell the Christian story of sex in its own way. *God is a lover who made us to love like him.* We're not in the business of forcing anyone to agree with us, but we do want to invite people into our beautiful vision for life—a vision that might seem crazy to them at first sight.

We want to explain that there's something more going on in our human story than DNA and hormones. We would love to unpack with them God's passionate, faithful, life-giving vision. Why though, is it worth them listening, particularly in the light of our chequered history in this area? Well, there is another side to the story.

Despite our obvious failings, Christianity has shaped the world we live in for the better over two millennia. It contains wisdom and insight into human nature and the good life that has crossed cultures and led to development throughout history and across the globe. Christians built the civilisation we westerners live in. They founded our democracies and developed our modern ideas of human rights, justice and compassionate care. They ended slavery and established universal education. And they were and are in the forefront of the fight against poverty, prejudice and ignorance.

Since its birth, Christianity has etched compassion into culture. The very first Christians provided extraordinary care for their community (see Acts 2 v 42-47; 6 v 1-7). They brought a sense of sacredness to childhood that was unknown in the pagan world. Christianity's commitment to reason and truth instead of mystery and intuition spurred on the development of science.[7]

More recently, the Cadbury family revolutionised factory working conditions from "dismal and dangerous" to "safe and humane", with decent pay, pensions, medical provision and training.[8] William Wilberforce campaigned to end the slave trade. Lord Shaftesbury attended his funeral and, as a member of the British Parliament went on to spearhead the regulation of child labour, care for the mentally ill and set up schools for homeless children.[9]

---

7   https://bit.ly/2LfPoht (Accessed 1st May 2019).

8   https://bit.ly/2HzDyvR (Accessed 1st May 2019).

9   https://bit.ly/2HBq6rA (Accessed 1st May 2019).

We could go on. But the key thing is that these efforts were always part of a package deal. The first Christians devoted themselves to the apostles teaching (Acts 2 v 42). Lord Shaftesbury said that in schools "the teaching of the Bible should be essential and not an extra." In other words justice, social progress and commitment to the teaching of the Christian faith went together.

So despite our failings, Christians don't simply point the finger—we roll up their sleeves. We support the addicted and abused, the weak and the vulnerable. We still seek to etch compassion into our communities. Women from local churches befriend and support sex-workers. Christians commend the intimate love of God that outshines and outlasts the matchstick lust of pornography. And Christians reach out to families going through painful break-ups.

One story I heard recently illustrated this really clearly. Sandra was a sex-worker who was approached by some Christian women when she was at a point of utter desperation. The women regularly visited where she worked to befriend and support her and the other workers there.

Sandra speaks with great kindness of the way they loved her, and provided hope in what seemed to her like a helpless situation. They linked her with support and helped her to get an National Insurance number. This meant that she was able to get other work and begin to save. With the money that she earned from this, she was eventually able to move back home to Eastern Europe and escape exploitation. Those Christians rolled up their sleeves to confront the effects of injustice.

In every culture, there are aspects of Christianity that grate against the majority view: things that make it seem distant and unbelievable. But a glance back at history should make us cautious about simply getting swept up in the mood of the moment.

For example, the rise of fascism was greeted by a wave of enthusiasm in the 1930s but now is widely seen as dangerous and flawed. Rather more mundanely, if you watch any old science-fiction movie, you will quickly see how their visions of the future just 20 or 30 years ago are remarkably out of date today. Perhaps these sorts of observation should at least make us ask if we are really sure that our 21st century Western view of the world is flawless?[10]

Reading Glynn Harrison's analysis of today's culture in *A Better Story* raised this issue starkly for me. Glynn is a Christian psychiatrist and academic who asked some searching questions and found surprising answers. His research shows that people are actually having *less* sex than before, are more lonely, and that, rather than experiencing liberation, women and children in particular face new vulnerabilities and threats to their flourishing. It made me question whether the sexual freedom that our culture promotes is really delivering what it seems to promise.

---

10 Timothy Keller, *The Reason for God* (Hodder and Stoughton, 2009) p 112.

If these observations create doubt, it is worth appealing to sceptics to give the Christian view a hearing. In fact, before discarding the Christian worldview in favour of relatively new and untested theories of gender and the family, I want to ask my friends to let me map out the Biblical vision "from the inside." I wonder if we can say something like "instead of just responding to 'hot button' issues, please will you allow me to outline the Christian case on its own terms. *God is a lover who made us to love like him* and everything we believe about sexuality stems from this."

We have another story to tell: a story that has its own inner logic and a radiant, attractive beauty to it. I hope in some small way this book has begun to point to God's big love story as a just and liberating vision for the flourishing of the whole world.

4. Never

The "never" is to remind us that there are some things that, for the Christian, are non-negotiable. We're thankful that we live in a society in which we are free to express them. We believe that everyone should have a right to live in a world where they are free to have different opinions.

Too often the majority voice wants to silence or ridicule anyone who thinks differently. Yet the opportunity to think our own thoughts is a precious gift. We won't always agree, but Christians want to protect the right of everyone to speak freely.

In our case, the big love story of God is our blueprint for life. We want to serve our friends, family, work colleagues and neighbours as much as we can. Compassion is etched into our communities. But we don't want people to admire us for these traits, but to ask us to tell them the big story.

God is a lover who made us to love like him. He gave us marriage to show us what that is like—passionate, faithful and life giving. A married person committed to Christ says *Yes!* to God's story by saying *No!* to the intimate advances of others: in other words, by sticking with their spouse. Just as Jesus sticks with us even at the cost of his life, we stick with the person we are married to.

The single person committed to Christ said *Yes!* to God's story by saying *No!* to sex outside marriage: in other words, by faithful abstinence. Just as Christ doesn't do one-night stands or fall out of love with his church, nor do we with him. When we live this out in communities filled with friendship we find that everyone can thrive— whether single, married, divorced or same-sex attracted.

How is this possible? In the end, our own sexual feelings are just the tip of the iceberg of God's big love story. There is something more. At the centre is Christ the bridegroom, who promises to marry his pure bride (Isaiah 54 v 5; Ephesians 5). He throws a huge reception and commits to eternal intimacy with her. And when he wants to describe this intimacy, he chooses sex to do so.

The sexual love shared by a married couple was always meant to point to something more—the quality of our relationship with Jesus Christ. There is no other vocabulary that can begin to communicate the depth, the richness and the intensity of the eternal intimacy that Jesus has in store for all who love him.

Swipe up

We will not let go of the love of God—the God who sees what I'm really like and decides to love me anyway. The Father who wants us to join in with the joyful ecstatic union he had with his Son and the Spirit before the world began. The Son who was prepared to die to make that happen. The Spirit who helps me to love like the triune God loves us day by day.

What we've seen of God has moved him in our estimation from an impersonal reference in history to a priceless personal Saviour. And what takes our breath away is that we've only scratched the surface. For us, to love like him is the key to our flourishing, and an honour we can never abandon.

Afterword

or Where to from here?

If you've been intrigued by this sketch of God's big vision for sexuality, and how it relates to where you are at, I'm sure you have questions, worries and concerns. Can I urge you brother, sister, not to ignore these, but to go deeper and reach out for support. The first thing to say is *please don't struggle alone.* Our loving God has made us part of a family so that we never have to bear burdens or face challenges alone. Find someone in your local church you can trust, with whom you can share your struggles and pray for wisdom together.

There may be things from the past that trouble you, relationships in the present that need a rethink, or hopes for the future that worry you. Please speak to your pastor or someone in leadership. They will be able to help you find more in-depth help.

I want to point you to some other resources that can help as well. Many of the ideas in this short book find their origin in a larger work by Glynn Harrison called *A Better Story: God, Sex and Human Flourishing* (IVP, 2017). For a more detailed look at where the ideas in our culture come from and how to think about them biblically, it's gold. Glynn also shows in detail how the promises and narratives of the sexual revolution are flawed and failing.

Glen Scrivener, the other friend with whom I chatted through the ideas of this book, has produced a brilliant six-minute video called "Why are Christians so weird about sex?" Search for the title on YouTube and watch it!

If you're single

For those who are trying to live out the "heavenly" part of God's love story as a single person, Kate Wharton's book *Single-Minded* is down to earth, honest and immensely practical. Whether you are same-sex attracted or not, the Living Out website (livingout.org) is also a great starting point. For answers to some of the questions that those who experience same-sex attraction raise, Ed Shaw's book *The Plausibility Problem* (IVP, 2013) is funny, readable and generally excellent.

Wes Hill's short but powerful books *Washed and Waiting* (Zondervan, 2016) and its sequel *Spiritual Friendship* (Brazos, 2015) are also worth reading. They take you on his journey of why he chooses to live a celibate single life and the resources he's used to stay faithful.

If you're married

For those wanting to strengthen their marriage, Rachel and I have found *What Did You Expect?* by Paul Tripp (IVP, 2012) and *Married for God* by Christopher Ash (IVP, 2007) particularly encouraging. Tim Keller's talks on marriage (available through www.gospelinlife.com) are really helpful in shaping our attitude and expectations too.

For your children

If you are wanting to begin to introduce your children to sex and sexuality in an age-appropriate way, we've used the *God's Design for Sex* series by Stan and Brenna Jones (NavPress, 2007). More recently Patricia Weerakoon's *Birds and Bees by the Book* (Youthworks, 2017) has been recommended to us. For older children and teens check out Sarah Smith's book *A Guide to Growing Up: how to have honest conversations with young people about puberty, sex and God* (Monarch, 2017). We've also been recommended *Growing up God's Way* by Chris Richards and Liz Jones (Evangelical Press, 2014).

Whatever else you do, keep returning to the Spring of living water, our ever Faithful friend. The One who sticks closer than a brother and promises pleasures for evermore: Jesus Christ.

the good book
COMPANY

BIBLICAL | RELEVANT | ACCESSIBLE

At The Good Book Company, we are dedicated to helping Christians and local churches grow. We believe that God's growth process always starts with hearing clearly what he has said to us through his timeless word—the Bible.

Ever since we opened our doors in 1991, we have been striving to produce Bible-based resources that bring glory to God. We have grown to become an international provider of user-friendly resources to the Christian community, with believers of all backgrounds and denominations using our books, Bible studies, devotionals, evangelistic resources, and DVD-based courses.

We want to equip ordinary Christians to live for Christ day by day, and churches to grow in their knowledge of God, their love for one another, and the effectiveness of their outreach.

Call us for a discussion of your needs or visit one of our local websites for more information on the resources and services we provide.

Your friends at The Good Book Company

thegoodbook.com | thegoodbook.co.uk
thegoodbook.com.au | thegoodbook.co.nz
thegoodbook.co.in